FROM
THE
CABLES of
GENOCIDE: *Poems on Love and Hunger*

*L*ORNA DEE CERVANTES

Arte Publico Press
Houston
Texas
1991

This book is made possible by a grant from the National Endowment for the Arts, a federal agency, and the Texas Commission on the Arts.

The author wishes to acknowledge the generous assistance of Clifton Reed and Stuart Presley, friends, housemates, writers/artists in their own right who helped to cover rent, utilities, and allowed their cupboards to be periodically raided by this hungry poet in 1988-89. Without their aid this collection would not have been possible thanks to no grants at all.

Please support the following publications where poems from this collection first appeared:

"Drawings" in ZYZZYVA 5.2; 41 Sutter, Suite 1400, San Francisco, CA 94104.

"The Poet Is Served Her Papers," "On Love and Hunger," "Colorado Blvd.," "The Captive's Verses," "Continental Divide" in The Americas Review 17.3-4; University of Houston, Houston TX 77204-2090.

"The Levee: Letter to No One," "Pleiades from the Cables of Genocide" in Frontiers 11.1; Women Studies programs, Univesity of Colorado, Boulder, CO 80309-0246.

"Raisins" in The Berkeley Poetry Review 21; 700 Eshleman Hall, University of California, Berkeley, CA 94720.

"The Last Meal" in Quarry West 24; and "To We Who Were Saved by the Stars," "Walking Around" in Quarry West 26: "Diálogo a Chicanas y Chicanos"; Porter College, University of California, Santa Cruz, CA 95064.

"Lápiz Azul" was first published in broadside form by Toothpaste Press, Iowa and by Humanizarte 9.1 along with "Le Petit Mal"; Centro Chicano de Escritores, 477 15th Street, Rm. 200, Oakland, CA 94612

"On the Fear of Going Down" in The Mid-American Review 10.1; 106 Hanna Hall, Department of English, Bowling Green State University, Bowling Green, OH 43403.

"Colorado" in Tonantzin September-October, 1990; guadalupe Cultural Arts Center, 1300 Guadalupe St., San Antonio, TX 78207-5519.

Recovering the past, creating the future

Arte Público Press
University of Houston
Houston, Texas 77204-2174

Cover design by Mark Piñón
Original painting by Diana Rodríguez Cárdenas: "Desasesinados," Copyright © 1989

Cervantes, Lorna Dee.
From the cables of genocide: poems on love and hunger / Lorna Dee Cervantes.
p. cm.
ISBN 1-55885-033-3
I. Title.
PS3553.E79F7 1991
811'.54-dc20   91-8721
                                                                        CIP

0 1 2 3 4 5 6 7 8 9   10 9 8 7 6 5 4 3

to Sylvia Plath, Frida Kahlo and Violeta Parra

and for J

*Freedom is expensive, but the price
is not impossible to pay.*

—Don Juan

Contents

From the Cables of Genocide:
Poems on Love and Hunger

I

———

From the Cables of Genocide

*If you had enough bad things
happen to you as a child you may
as well kiss off the rest of your life.*

—an anonymous mental health worker

Drawings: For John Who Said
to Write about True Love

"The writer. It's a cul-de-sac," you wrote that
winter of our nation's discontent. That first time
I found you, blue marble lying still in the trench, you, staked
in waiting for something, anything but the cell of your small
apartment with the fixtures never scrubbed, the seven great
named cats you gassed in the move. *I couldn't keep them.*
You explained so I understood. And what cat never loved
your shell-like ways, the claw of your steady fingers, *firme*
from the rasping of banjos and steady as it goes
from the nose to the hair to the shaking tip. My favorite
tale was of the owl and the pussycat in love in a china cup
cast at sea, or in a flute more brittle, more lifelike
and riddled with flair, the exquisite polish of its gaudy
glaze now puzzled with heat cracks, now foamed
opalescent as the single espresso dish you bought from
Goodwill. What ever becomes of the heart our common
child fashioned, red silk and golden satin, the gay glitter
fallen from moves, our names with *Love* written in black
felt pen? Who gets what? Who knows what becomes of the
rose you carried home from Spanish Harlem that morning
I sat waiting for the surgeon's suction. What ever becomes
of waiting and wanting, when the princess isn't ready and
the queen has missed the boat, again? Do you still write
those old remarks etched on a page of Kandinsky's ace
letting go? Like: *Lorna meets Oliver North and she
kicks his butt.* The dates are immaterial to me as
salvation or a freer light bending through stallions
in an air gone heavy with underground tunnels. Do you
read me? Is there some library where you'll find me, smashed
on the page of some paper? *Let it go* is my morning mantra
gone blind with the saved backing of a clock, now dark
as an empty womb when I wake, now listening for your tick
or the sound of white walls on a sticky street. Engines out
the window remind me of breathing apparatus at the breaking
of new worlds, the crash and perpetual maligning of the sand
bar where sea lions sawed up logs for a winter cabin. I dream
wood smoke in the morning. I dream the rank and file of used

up chimneys, what that night must have smelled like, her mussed
and toweled positioning, my ambulance of heart through stopped
traffic where you picked the right corner to tell me: *They think*
someone murdered her. You were there, all right, you were
a statue carved from the stone of your birth. You were patient
as a sparrow under leaf and as calm as the bay those light
evenings when I envisioned you with the fishwife you loved.
And yes, I could have done it then, kissed it off, when the scalpel
of single star brightened and my world blazed, a dying bulb
for the finger of a socket, like our sunsets on the Cape, fallen
fish blood in snow, the hearts and diamonds we found and left
alone on a New England grave. Why was the summer so long
then? Even now a golden season stumps me and I stamp
ants on the brilliant iced drifts. I walk a steady mile
to that place where you left it, that solid gold band
thrown away to a riptide in a gesture the theatrical
love—so well. What was my role? Or did I leave it
undelivered when they handed me the gun of my triggered
smiles and taught me to cock it? Did I play it to the hilt
and bleeding, did I plunge in your lap and wake to find you
lonely in a ribbon of breathing tissue? Does this impudent
muscle die? Does love expire? Do eternal nestings mean much
more than a quill gone out or the spit? I spy the bank
of frothed fog fuming with airbrushed pussies on a pink
horizon. I score my shoes with walking. My skill is losing.
It's what we do best, us ducks, us lessons on what not
to do.
                    Thanks for the crack,

                                        you wrote
in my O.E.D. that 30th renewal when the summer snapped
and hissed suddenly like a bullet of coal flung from a fire
place or a dumb swallow who dove into the pit for pay. Kiss
her, and it's good luck. I palm this lucky trade but the soot
never sells and I never sailed away on a gulf stream that divides
continents from ourselves. But only half of me is cracked, the
other is launched on a wild bob, a buoy, steadfast in storm. I may
sail to Asia or I might waft aimlessly to Spain where my hemp
first dried from the rain. My messages wring from the line,
unanswered, pressed sheets from an old wash or the impression
of a holy thing. But don't pull no science on this shroud, the
date will only lie. She'll tell you it's sacred, even sell you
a piece of the fray. She appears on the cracked ravines of this

country like a ghost on the windshield of an oncoming
train. She refuses to die, but just look at her nation
without a spare penny to change. My wear is a glass made
clean through misuse, the mishandling of my age as revealing
as my erased face, Indian head of my stick birth, my battle
buried under an island of snow I've yet to get to. What could I do
with this neighborhood of avenues scattered with empty shells
of mailboxes, their feet caked with cement like pulled up
pilings? Evidently, they haven't a word
                                        for regret
                                                full heart.
Someday, I said, I can write us both from this mess. But the key
stalls out from under me when I spell your name. I have to fake
the O or go over it again in the dark, a tracing of differences
spilled out on a sheet. If I could stick this back
together, would it stay? It's no rope, I know, and no good
for holding clear liquid. I gather a froth on my gums, and grin
the way an old woman grimaces in a morning mirror. I was never
a clear thing, never felt the way a daughter feels, never lost
out like you, never drove. My moon waits at the edge
of an eagle's aerie, almost extinct and the eggs are fragile
from poisoned ignitions. I'm never coming out from my cup
of tea, never working loose the grease in my hair, the monkey
grease from my dancing elbows that jab at your shoulder.
But I write, and wait for the book to sell, for I know
nothing comes of it but the past with its widening teeth,
with its meat breath baited at my neck, persistent as the smell
of a drunk. Don't tell me. I already know. It's just the rule of
the game for the jack of all hearts, and for the queen of baguettes;
it's a cul-de-sac for a joker drawing hearts.

Persona Ingrata

It didn't matter
that the summer swelled
and lit like paper streaming
from an ember of dying light.

It didn't matter
that the phrases of a wish
phased out and your face,
lit by coal, was etched
by a waif's tremulous rivers.

It didn't matter
when the waves bore holes
in our belonging and the shallows
hollowed out on desire or the sea
with its bedlam of hammers and sirens
fell apart one day as the pelican, beak
sawed in half by suicide, hungers.

What does it matter,
the ash our legacies cover?
This no receipt for buying time?
This loving on lease, paid
through the much-obliged heart?

Does it matter?
This ring in my ears
culling my sleep? This silence
when I move through you
that succumbs me
when I least expect it?
This slaughtering autumn
that overbears and intensifies
the falling out of constellations?

Would it matter if
my memory wouldn't lie,
wouldn't treat me with neglect?
Or if my sudden plunge into

an element you despise wouldn't
quicken me or paralyze
into dry leaving off?

It matters
when the crow calls,
when it flies to the left
of you, when the sea's
sliced sun follows you
like a boat in pursuit, and
despair of yellowed things
crusts at your insides.

It matters
when the feather of a kiss
at your nape stuns fate
into destiny or sorrow
at the gate gives up —

a simple matter
to matter as you
mean to me.

The Levee: Letter to No One

Today I watched a woman by the water
cry. She looked like my mother: red
stretch pants, blue leisure top,
her hair in a middle-age nest egg.
She wiped her face, her only act
for old tears, slow as leftover piss.
She was there a long, long time,
sitting on the levee, her legs swinging
like a young girl's over sewer spew.
She slapped her cheeks damp.
I wondered what she watched:
blue herons, collapsing and unfolding
in the tulles, half lips of lapping river
foam, the paper of an egret's tail?
Does she notice beauty? Does she notice
the absence of swallows, the knife
of their throats calling out dusk?
Does she notice the temporary
denial of fish, the flit of silver
chains flung from a tern, the drop
of their dive? Funny, we use the sound
slice to imitate the movement
of hunger through wind or waves.
A slice of nothing as nothing
is ever separate in the realm of this
element. Only symmetry harbors loss,
only the fusion of difference
can be wrenched apart, divorced
or distanced from its source.
I walked the levee back both sides
after that. The river is a good place
for this silt and salt, this reservoir,
depository bank, for piss
and beauty's flush.

The Poet Is Served Her Papers

So tell me about fever dreams,
about the bad checks we scrawl
with our mouths, about destiny
missing last bus to oblivion.

I want to tell lies
to the world and believe it.
Speak easy, speak spoken to,
speak lips opening on a bed of nails.

Hear the creaking of cardboard
in these telling shoes?
The mint of my mind
gaping far out of style?

Hear the milling of angels
on the head of a flea?
My broke blood is sorrel, is a lone
mare, is cashing in her buffalo chips.

As we come to the cul-de-sac
of our heart's slow division
tell me again about true
love's bouquet, paint hummingbird

hearts taped to my page.
Sign me over with XXXs
and *passion*. Seal on the lick
of a phone, my life. And pay.

And pay. And pay.

Santa Cruz

So what of our sputtering names,
unhinged. So what of blank
seasons, blistered and shot
from the cannons of our slow desires.

And what of summer's pestilence,
our worried flies on sweat sand?
What of the harbor where we fished
our love seals into mute extinction?

What will become of the kiss
I give you, the spit on my lip,
the lips of my vulva pushing
fins and flash? Twelve bushels

of silt and salt, this year
I rivet on a tide as gray
as winter and it stops
my catch. What about the graves

where the suds first dug apart
the sloughs of our nesting?
See the slit-throat pelicans,
the dumbed whales beached on cape foam?

What of this poet
reading season's end?
My worm heart, overwrought
as a slacked line, loses.

Litost

I keep hoping she'll die but I think
it's me with my lumps at the breast, heart
stalled on a dare, growing exclusion at the base
of my vase. Your roses, please, but the note renders
in a foreign calligraphy, some webbing of duck
feet dangling from the noose like a yanked ginseng
man. I keep hoping he'll die, that man who keeps her
from you, who keeps parting the curvature of the earth
as seasons slug on, forgetting, stalking, colliding
like cars against the calendar of your steady
ruling. Show me a map where the countries
aren't women. I know all about us exotics
in the hot house of your dreams. I watch
a spiderwoman as she beats up the bitch.
Rita Hayworth, she had it coming!
as I pummel the distance between us
into nothing. And nothing works.
And what don't work won't fix.
I pick up the thread, what's left of
grandma's chain-of-hearts, and the clay feet
of the pot it's stuck in, bonsai to the bone, I break it
at the neck as I look at her, spitting spiders of blood.

*Litost is a word with no exact translation ... a feeling that is the synthesis of many
others: grief, sympathy, remorse, and an undefinable longing.
Litost is a state of torment caused by a sudden insight into one's own miserable self.
First comes a feeling of torment, then the desire for revenge.*

—Milan Kundera

Politeness Takes Her Turn

At the fifth reconciliation
I have my primal scene, I act
the dream: in walks the bitch
pristine as Rita Hayworth's rival,
luminescent teeth and nails, hair
her wind has never bit, the skinny
stature of her single grace.
How do you stand it?
she drawls, and quakes.
Furniture is first to go,
camp chair to barren 'fridge,
the desk, the lamp I wrenched
from work. Yes. It's the little
things we do that mean a lot:
the china cup my mother bought
(parasoled decadence), no good
for lips, unholdable tub shape.
Little bland girls.
It shatters in the kitchen
where I steady paced
my web of midnights, drilled
my path of cauldron recipes
and moored in the shadow
of their receipts. I smile
at her. I answer:
You call this standing?

The House He Falls in Love With

> *... not time, but space; memory:*
> *the irrecoverable home.*
>
> —Paul Zweig

Its greatest virtue is how it hides its emptiness.
It bears the face of solitude's continence in gray
facade. The soulful eyes, windowseats at the front,
see you from three sides. They open into darkness
and minute divisions of light at the inner eye, a
patchwork of sky and treeline taken up by the panes
of north at the inside rear. Every opening
is another opening, a Chinese box of a house.
All doors and windows. The rest is geometry.
Nothing really. Nothing more to see
than the third eye at the top with its sill,
a chimney where a poet might imagine ignitions
of fireflies, a white rail of teeth on the shy
smile of a diffident stairwell that splits,
that comes in and lets out like a tide.
It can go either way. It's a sure bet.
Small, mostly latticework around the bottom
underworld, a secret stature that bolsters
an empty shell built for an island.
House for sale. There for the asking.
Your property for a price.

Valentine

Cherry plums suck a week's soak,
overnight they explode into the scenery of before
your touch. The curtains open on the end of our past.
Pink trumpets on the vines bare to the hummingbirds.
Butterflies unclasp from the purse of their couplings, they
light and open on the doubled hands of eucalyptus fronds.
They sip from the pistils for seven generations that bear
them through another tongue as the first year of our
punishing mathematic begins clicking the calendar
forward. They land like seasoned rocks on the
decks of the cliffs. They take another turn
on the spiral of life where the blossoms
blush & pale in a day of dirty dawn
where the ghost of you webs
your limbs through branches
of cherry plum. Rare bird,
extinct color, you stay in
my dreams in x-ray. In
rerun, the bone of you
stripping sweethearts
folds and layers the
shedding petals of
my grief into a
decayed holo-
gram—my
for ever
empty
art.

II

——

On Love and Hunger

People tell me I sing the words
'love' and 'hunger' like no one else.
Well, everything I know is wrapped
up in those two words. You've got
to have something to eat and a little
love in your life before you can hold
still for anybody's damned sermon.

—Billie Holliday

My Dinner with Your Memory

A woman's scent is nothing
like bread, although sometimes I steam
when the moon slivers my heart
into poverty's portions. This one's
for you, though you lie, though you deserve
none of this butter. On the table between
us: a slab of meat that once tasted
cud the size of my breast, a cunning
wire to slip off some cheese, a plum
brandy that dissolves into nothing, silver
on the tongue as that talk we devour.
Who would hunger at the brink of this
feast? Who would go, uninvited,
but you and your ghost of a dog?

Raisins

Raisins are my currency
to date—slightly seedy,
prickled as my nipples,
black as pubis, colored
as my opened eyelids.
I tongue you
fricatives into vowels.
I suck you
to the scabs
you were, forbidden
fruit. Reminders.
Never mind
the way I found you
deserted in the depot
stall. No matter
how this small red box
was once a child's.
Lost wonder, you're
the gift of grace
swept up off
the bathroom floor.
You're my only food
today, the day I left
you, paper husband,
widowed name.
Our final meal
was sweet, you
hovered over me,
an empty package,
beating blades
to froth, teething
me the way I like it,
both lips bit and shriveled
as our last fuck you.   .
You are black with rust
and will restore my blood.
You're my prize of faith,
stave against starve.
I eat it. Grateful

for the brief exchange.
Twenty eight tips
of fate. Three good sweats
they soaked in sun
as you now soak
my spit, sweet as acid, damp as rot.
This hunger, as your
memory, feeds
by chance.

Night Stand

'Onions, lettuce, leeks, broccoli,
garlic, cantaloupe, peaches, plums ... '

The man whose work is hard
slides onto me glistening
as a bass wielding the sheen
I'm mirrored with when I
step out of the bath.
He wears the patch the sun
has x-rayed to his chest.
He's the color of work.
I'm the color of reading.
I hold my sembrador
under the august calabasas
of his arms. As first
light drifts through gauze
I have eyes the half wild
know with: half bitch,
half wolf; here I am
extraterritorial
in the divisions,
extinctual as a missing
lynx. Its a foreign well
I drag my sullen bucket to—
in a western bar on a frontage
road where we recognize the past
and find we have escaped the thing
which in the night would eat us.

We are gouged by the machinery,
we fill the holes with fire.
We pull the pails another sloshing
day up through the cracks in our
overdue finality. He is wearing
hundred dollar shoes, wool slacks,
linen. He's making better money
now filling holes and digging.
A better life for less is lost.

But if the dirt where I was born
still tamped beneath my feet, if
the concrete avalanche of progress
hadn't filled my love and the
rivers of my youth hadn't iced me
into middle age, I might have
stayed. But no
one stays.

His touch is like a man's
despite his age. His Moorish
fur, his Saturn eyes, his sadness
says: although he may not know
beyond the suicide of soul
the poor possess, the threshing race
machines, the names of Goerring,
Himmler, Buchenwald, Farben ...
and all that written fables
spell for us—this he knows—
Esta gente no entiende nada.

And I—am the way I had intended.
I've come to what I wanted.
And here, writing, wearing things
the discarded dead have
bought and sold: we know.

On Love and Hunger

*You can want to do nothing then de-
cide instead to do this: make leek soup, I
mean. Between the will to do something
and the will to do nothing is a thin, un-
changing line: suicide.*

—Marguerite Duras, "Leek Soup"

I feed you
as you hunger.
I hunger
as you feed
and refuse
the food I give.

Hunger is the first sense.
Imagination is the last.
You are my sixth sense,
imaginary lover,
missed meal.

Food is first choice,
first flaw, fatal
in its accessibility,
fearless on the tongue
of mean denial.

First word.
First sight.

Food is love
in trust.

On Speaking to the Dead

Did you love them enough?
Did you see the limned quartz
of their eyes? Are they in
their heavy beds? Is the sleeping
beast you call your heart
alive? They will eat
the night. They will burrow
out with spittle and tell tales
in twitching sockets. It will last
as long as paper or the cum
cry of our living. Guilt.
It's like this: an oratory
of ants begins on the crested
graves. The dutiful
survive with grace, holding
granite in their weighty
mandibles. Lined like ants,
the red and black surmise,
orderly, filed, and eat
the heart that ails them.

Flatirons

for the Ute and Arapaho

The mountains are there like ghosts
of slaughtered mules, the whites of my
ancestors rest on the glaciers, veiled
and haloed with the desire of electrical
storms. Marginal feasts corral the young
to the cave walls, purple smoke wafts up
a chimney of shedding sundown. Statuesque
and exquisitely barren, my seed shines
in the dying rays. The rich earth of the wealthy
splays the legs of heaven in my view. Monstrous
and sullen, the slabs of death let loose their
hikers, let fall with an old snow. My harmony
of blood and ash, fire on the mound, I feel
them shuffling in the aspen, their vague ahems
marry the sucking fish in a derelict river. The
winter of their genocide still Ghost Dances
with a dream where the bison and mammoth unite,
where the story of their streams is as long
as the sabers of northern ice. The mountains
are the conquest of the sea, the belly of gems,
her fossil stays, her solicitudes. The glass
before the angel fish, she stands royal in
her invisible captivity, the impassability of her
element, elemental and efficient. She is there
in the silent baying, in the memory of a native
and the dripping pursuance of thawing babies—
specters in a sunset on The Heights—after massacre.

Death Song

The closer I come to death
the more the stuff of sex
rubs off, the harder stiff
sticks scrub cicada songs
of fury. Like scrawny
white cells breaking loose,
the dandruff of my days,
my doggone days,
works dry. My avalanche,
unfold me, work me free,
untooth me from the mountain
of this meadow: white sheets,
wrecked love, demure demeaning
slush. You save. And
the body bears its choice.

Abortion

Who is that keeps
knocking on the body?
She doesn't use the telephone
of dreams. He doesn't drive
into town on the freeway
writ of passage. This mail
leaves no forwarding address,
kicks around in the dust
like a fish who insists
on swimming into no one.
Who is this heavy hitcher
who keeps riding the bed
of my flat-handed hunger?
Doesn't she know, there's no one
at home? Doesn't he believe
this exit's not the last?

Colorado

She asks the man who is absent
if he might send her a photo
she can light before the candle
that keeps holding its breath
and won't stay lit for a prayer.
She sets a glass of water
on the shelf beside the bed
dirty with sweat. She lights
the match once more and once
again what is used up stays dark,
a virulent wick set in the mouth
of the jar. The water governs air
in the crusts of its sides, proof
of the existence of brujas, the owl
outside midnight and the feather
that flares when lit by ritual
desire vague as dreaming. She
empties the glass each morning
but can't get rid of the hex of hair
falling across his face when she turns
to the door, to the dead red clay.

Hotel

for John

I couldn't see in this light
even if I wished. The black
grillwork over black, cool upon coal,
kisses me back in an icy press.
Not wanting—anything—but to fall
as the empty trash cans mingle
below with the smell of feral cats.

Flailing moon the color of suds
over this factory of artifice,
moored in the poverty of my untouched
element, downed like a dog
struck by a diesel—one headlamp
flaring before my shadow's dust
buries its past in a crescent of mirth.

Lost now in this anonymity of barely
knowing you, my body would go
unsearched for in the rubble. Who could
remember my odor, my perfect strangeness
at a glance? Life leaves through the gate
of an ache, where you are, a vanishing
landscape. Do I dare it back?

I don't know where you go
anymore when you escape
into that vast wilderness
of our legal separation. Your
memory rises from the knocking
pipes, a sudden heat, a blast
of blood. Where does it go?

The galloping horses I hear are not
hooves but my heart kicking in its swollen
stall. But you, you take things as
a letting go, like a beacon that opens
a lens cap to our past. You take off
the dark like this snow-strewn alley,
a radiance, but no light of mine.

Jealous as an abandoned child, I
had no word for *father*. It floated
in heaven like *friend* or *famine*.
It rose like a muscle and punctuated
my dreams, the ones of ruined houses,
of countries like this one where the faces
of whores and the working poor are my own.

You had Irish eyes the color of old
ice. What you lost was first love
and a word for *forever*, like *evergreen*,
oceanic, fossil. My bones could grind
themselves to salt and I would still be
this aging woman, this battered lifeline.
History never has been kind to a loser.

What do I see when morning
chops ice into jade? What ring
could I trade now for the freedom
to bleed? What would I remember
of a hearth where the flags
of my silks beat at half mast, where
I studied a sure vocabulary of snow?

I had to leave before I could
hear it: the sound of dishwater
in a steamed house, the singing
of water on white porcelain, cooling
like clots seeping through a wound,
our collision of tensions, a viscous
rendered fat, divorced, releasing.

Colorado Blvd.

I wanted to die so I walked
the streets. Dead night,
black as iris, cold as the toes
on a barefoot drunk. Not a sound
but my shoes asking themselves over:
What season is this? Why is the wind
stuttering in its stall of nightmares?
Why courage or the bravery
of dripping steel? Given branches
rooted to their cunning, a kind
of snow lay fallow upon the hearth
of dried up trunks, wan and musing
like an absent guitarist strumming
wildly what she's forgotten most.
Bats fell about me like fire
or dead bark from my brow beaten
autumn. A kind of passing through
and when it called, the startled bird
of my birth, I left it, singing,
or fallen from its nest, it was silent
as the caves of my footfalls left
ridden in their absent burials.
What good was this? My cold
hearing, nothing, more desire
than protection. When would it come?
In that clove of cottonwood, perhaps
that shape in the mist, secret
as teeming lions? Is it my own
will that stalks me? Is it in
the slowed heart of my beatings
or the face that mists when
I least expect it? Frost covered
the windshields of the left
behind autos. In his parking
lot, my savior rests, lighting
his crack pipe, semi-automatic
poised at my nipple or the ear
I expose to witches and thieves:
Here it is. Will you kill for it?

On Touring Her Hometown

I'm going away to where I'm from.
I'm fleeing from visions, fences
grinning from the post. Give me
a hole with a past to it. Fill up
this mess with your wicked engines.
Give me the gun of holidays, calendar
shards, disarray on the avenues
unending as the streets of my vast
memory. There are marigolds six feet
under. They eat the names of the dead.
There are hovels under these caverns
where liquids marry and paint themselves
a mauve display. There's a place
in the mists of this city where a silence,
lean as ghosts, beckons, is archaic
in the workclothes of my otherness.
There is cedar, ash sage, an owl
on the grave of this town the width
of sin. And crying's like hating,
it won't ever pay. I'm going away
to where I'm from. I'm leaving,
last condor, last chance.

To We Who Were Saved by the Stars

Education lifts man's sorrows to a higher plane of regard.
A man's whole life can be a metaphor.

—Robert Frost

Nothing has to be ugly. Luck of the dumb
is a casual thing. It gathers its beauty in plain
regard. Animus, not inspiration, lets us go
among the flocks and crows crowded around
the railroad ties. Interchanges of far away
places, tokens of our deep faux pas, our interface
of neither/nor, when we mutter moist goodbye and ice
among the silent stars, it frosts our hearts on
the skids and corners, piles the dust upon our grids
as grimaces pardon us, our indecision, our monuments
to presidents, dead, or drafted boys who might have
married us, Mexican poor, or worse. Our lives could be
a casual thing, a reed among the charlatan drones,
a rooted blade, a compass that wields a clubfoot
round and round, drawing fairy circles in clumps
of sand. Irritate a simple sky and stars fill up
the hemispheres. One by one, the procession
of their birth is a surer song than change
jingling in a rich man's pocket. So knit, you
lint-faced mothers, tat your black holes
into paradise. Gag the grin that forms
along the nap. Pull hard, row slow, a white
boat to your destiny. A man's whole life
may be a metaphor—but a woman's lot
is symbol.

Pleiades from the Cables of Genocide

for my grandmother and against the budgets of '89

Tonight I view seven sisters
As I've never seen them before, brilliant
In their dumb beauty, pockmarked
In the vacant lot of no end winter
Blight. Seven sisters, as they were before,
Naked in a shroud of white linen, scented angels
Of the barrio, hanging around for another smoke,
A breath of what comes next, the aborted nest.
I'll drink to that, says my mother within. Her mother
Scattered tales of legendary ways when earth
Was a child and satellites were a thing of the
Heart. Maybe I could tell her this. I saw them
Tonight, seven Hail Marys, unstringing;
                            viewed Saturn
Through a singular telescope. Oh wonder
Of pillaged swans! oh breathless geometry
Of setting! You are radiant in your black light
Height, humming as you are in my memory,
Nights as inked as these, breathless
From something that comes from nothing.
Cold hearts, warm hands in your scuffed
Up pockets. I know the shoes those ladies wear,
Only one pair, and pointedly out of fashion
And flared-ass breaking at the toes, at the point
Of despair. Those dog gone shoes. No repair
For those hearts and angles, minus of meals, that
Flap through the seasons, best in summer, smelling
Of sneakers and coconuts, armpits steaming
With the load of the lording boys who garnish
Their quarters: the gun on every corner,
A chamber of laughter as the skag
Appears—glossed, sky white and sunset
Blush, an incandescence giving out, giving up
On their tests, on their grades, on their sky
Blue books, on the good of what's right. A star,
A lucky number that fails all, fails math, fails
Street smarts, dumb gym class, fails to jump
Through the broken hoop, and the ring

Of their lives wounds the neck not their
Arterial finger. Seven sisters, I knew them
Well. I remember the only constellation
My grandmother could point out with the punch
Of a heart. My grandma's amber stone
Of a face uplifts to the clarity of an eaglet's
Eye—or the vision of an águila
Whose mate has succumbed, and she uplifts
Into heaven, into their stolen hemispheres.
                                        It is true.
When she surrenders he will linger by her leaving,
Bringing bits of food in switchblade talons, mice
For the Constitution, fresh squirrel for her wings
The length of a mortal. He will die there, beside
Her, belonging, nudging the body into the snowed
Eternal tide of his hunger. Hunters will find them
Thus, huddled under their blankets of aspen
Leaves. Extinct. And if she lives who knows what
Eye can see her paused between ages and forgotten
Stories of old ways and the new way
Of ripping apart. They are huddled, ever squaring
With the division of destiny. You can find them
In the stars, with a match, a flaring of failure,
That spark in the heart that goes out with impression,
That thumb at the swallow's restless beating.
And you will look up, really to give up, ready
To sail through your own departure. I know.
My grandmother told me, countless times, it was all
She knew to recite to her daughter of daughters,
Her Persephone of the pen.
                          The Seven Sisters
Would smoke in the sky in their silly shoes
And endless waiting around doing nothing,
Nothing to do but scuff up the Big Bang with salt
And recite strange stories of epiphanies of light,
Claim canons, cannons and horses, and the strange
Men in their boots in patterns of Nazis and Negroes.
I count them now in the sky on my abacus of spun duck
Lineage, a poison gas. There, I remind me, is the nation
Of peace: seven exiles with their deed of trust
Signed over through gunfire of attorney.
                              She rides

Now through the Reagan Ranch her mothers owned.
I know this—we go back to what we have loved
And lost. She lingers, riding in her pied pinto gauchos,
In her hat of many colors and her spurs, her silver
Spurs. She does not kick the horse. She goes
Wherever it wants. It guides her to places where
The angry never eat, where birds are spirits
Of dead returned for another plot or the crumb
Of knowledge, that haven of the never to get.
And she is forever looking to the bare innocence
Of sky, remembering, dead now, hammered as she is
Into her grave of stolen home. She is singing
The stories of Calafia ways and means, of the nacre
Of extinct oysters and the abalone I engrave
With her leftover files. She knows the words
To the song now, what her grandmother sang
Of how they lit to this earth from the fire
Of fusion, on the touchstones of love tribes. *Mira,*
She said, *This is where you come from.* The power
                              peace
Of worthless sky that unfolds me—now—in its greedy
Reading: Weeder of Wreckage, Historian of the Native
Who says: *It happened. That's all. It just happened.*
And runs on.

The Chumash who inhabited the Santa Barbara coast may have believed that they descended to earth from the Pleiades, also known as The Seven Sisters.
The Seven Sisters also refers to the seven big oil companies.

III

The Captive's Verses

Enemy, my enemy,
has love fallen to dust
and will nothing do save flesh and bone furiously adored
while the fire devours itself
and the red harnessed horses rush into hell?

—Pablo Neruda

Europa and Calafia

Sea moss and evergreen, glistening
Agate and dollar-sized kelp on the rocks,
How much it costs—this holding on,
This five fingered squeeze on the cracks.

Europa and Calafia sleep
In the shadow of liquid
Lost between two blades
Fragrant with mis-desire.

In the clearing of waves
Arbors of whales twist in the spray,
Dolphins lace among the schools and
An abundance sails amid symmetries.

Two figures drowse through centuries;
I have felt her shiver and rouse
A nap of redwoods from her sleeve, and
Beneath me she rises in my bones.

You summon the other, like a shadow
Of light she appears at your window
Golden and speechless, same age
As death, she sings through your pencil.

Fine as an eyelid, these fragile
Crusts endure. Water and a memory
Of birth wills us to dream: the flood
Or the fish greater than the rest.

We lie as two choices. Europa
And Calafia sleep, their calligraphy
Of coast defines the banking surf:
No limits but air, effort and earth.

The Captive's Verses

after Neruda

There is another side to you
un lago where the huesos
border in ripples of hot
and cold water, mammal

breath upon the hair of your
chest, chrysanthemums
in your ears, your pods,
stellular. I would tell

of another isle, another gill
upon the shark's fin of you,
an infestation of expectations.
Espíritus. Adelantes. Bury

it all! Gold upon break.
You are Captain of it all.
And me, the ship's booty.
You are brave. Decay.

I'm left my cunning. My
country ruined. My nation
wasted. My wash of it
left wringing in the mud.

My bloodmeal seals the crop.
There is this side to you:
He who doesn't give her
any pleasure but triggers it,

cocksure by doubt. By love
I swear by it.
Bite by it.
Swear.

Plenos Poderes

after Neruda

Does it fill you with power,
with water, with stone,
to create a want so ceaseless?
Hear the creaking of moon

as she reaches to sea, hair
full of shimmering jellies
and diatoms lost in the craters?
There's a skull and crossbones

in the fix of the rip, in the breakers
incessant breaking of cradle and rock.
All night, all tide, solstice to solstice,
she bends and bears the bending

of water as you filled me with child
so I felt I would give birth to it.
What do I do with the key
to this city, this door to you

that never opened fully?
Do I change my life into yours?
Do I do what the women dare?
Do I abort it? Now that the earth

rusts with the weight of it?
Do I love you less? Do I spit
in the moon's single eye?
Do I survive? Do I? Plenos poderes

and singing.

Le Petit Mal

after Neruda

Love, if I die
how do I explain it?
Birds harbor mites
between their breasts

and who knows it?
Who speaks the dark
secret of secretive
dark arbors? Were I a bird

I would be a feather
of a bird, as light
as ash upon your gone
brow, the furrow of lisp

over the fur of your
lips. I would take
my advantage of you,
beetle my legs between

yours. Do all lonesome
penance before the sentence
of your name. Say special
grace to your hope

chest, quake before
thin mountains of
rivering, feathering,
full now, a waking

bird, my murmuring heart,
my quiver and arrow;
my shot—I'm shot
full of you. Dead.

Lápiz Azul

A blast of the bluest
air—my jay sears
across free clouds
with sheer audacity.
I love you like this.
A swoop of the heart
and there it is—a field
so blue I live through
a dense dream of wet
and white. This world
could be a dream, this
dream, a universe.
This season's flight
I go, holding an in-
efficient compass
of pure heart. Love,
I can't tell you
how it is to dissolve
out of duty and air
and the thick grief
of the expendable.

Y Volver

Who is to say Love
with her battered face
won't come? Who's to know
she won't rise and run
her comb through clotted
hair and spray the scent
of mysterious apples
between her breasts?

She rises with the strength
of seeds and the rule of roots
riddling the sidewalk.
She is the hag who cries
for hours in the mewing
of lovers. She's the catch
in their sweaty breath,
the blush of rose wine
on the magnolia in winter.

She is her best in ice
when her swelling abides
and small mirrors litter
the lawns. She is the face
you casually scuff through
in the refuse of a storm.
She can't ever hear you
but she sings. She feeds

the blooming magpie
death until he's bloated
with the feast of her
leaving. She is the dried
blood gracing his wings.
Vengeful and forgiving,
her honor weighs in a few
blown stars, in the halo
that lingers in the west
when the launched nightship

explodes, in the one lie
she espouses in her heat,
the beat between her thighs,
the veldt where she holds
you when you mean to go
free. Love, in her candor,
can't explain the attraction
but nuzzles the wild
horse's mane, and rides.

"Love of My Flesh, Living Death"

after García Lorca

Once I wasn't always so plain.
I was strewn feathers on a cross
of dune, an expanse of ocean
at my feet, garlands of gulls.

Sirens and gulls. They couldn't tame you.
You know as well as they: to be
a dove is to bear the falcon
at your breast, your nights, your seas.

My fear is simple, heart-faced
above a flare of etchings, a lineage
in letters, my sudden stare. It's you.

It's you! sang the heart upon its mantel
pelvis. Blush of my breath, catch
of my see—beautiful bird—It's you.

Macho

Slender, you are, secret as rail
under a stairwell of snow, slim
as my lips in the shallow hips.

I had a man of gristle and flint,
fingered the fine lineament of flexed
talons under his artifice of grit.

Every perfect body houses force
or deception. Every calculated figure
fears the summing up of age.

You're a beautiful mess of thread and silk,
a famous web of work and waiting, an
angular stylus with the patience of lead.

Your potent lure links hunger to flesh
as a frail eagle alights on my chest,
remember: the word for *machismo* is *real*.

Ode to a Ranger

after Neruda

My poet, my fisherman, my lifesaver,
you are freon and ice with the substance
of snow, you, with the bleached wheat
grazing your breath-house.

With my bait and bare bones
I gather your rail. I vibrate
and drum with an inner lightning
listening to your blood talk.

Voyager of elusive passages,
caster of the line and lure, you,
with the silences you never complete,
with your falling net of clothing:

Are you filling in the blanks
on your reports? Are you towing
in the pleasure boats? Uprighting
sunken sails? Am I your sudden accident?

Or paperwork undone? Am I peeling
invisible scales from your reticence?
Should I wet my hands before I touch you?
Is this muscular bullet in the shadows

you muskellunge? Freckle-Back,
German Brown, I am ironing the insignia
off your badges. I'm dissolving hooks,
ripping apart the dreaming gills

only to watch you slither upriver.
This is no catch and release provision.
This is my heart alarming the banks
of its dam. These are my hands

leading me over pastures of silt
from the factories of our muscles
and heat. Beautiful sailor, marshal
of my shallow shoal, what could I love

if not your eyes or the silent house
you wear? My savior of the wild
who would rather die, cold as copper
death to touch; my solitary range,

my pen.

Daffodils

for Jay

Verde, que te quiero verde.

—Federico García Lorca

It is true—I love
the daffodil, her succulent
radiation. *All things yellow
are good*, the Pueblo people say.
You are blue corn, the color
of the north vein that travels your thigh.
You are blue, the color of new dawn
when the pendulums of the earth desist,
when your love rises from her bed of stones,
and desire, desire's the sleepwalk of the beast.

I want—it is true—a stalk
of the wheat that grows on your breath-tomb,
which covers your bones, fine as the long
nails that girdle this flower. Green
que te quiero verde and the magic
of fingers digging their way into life,
leaves gone yellow from winter on the willow
tree. My branches are the arms that hold,
my hands complete the river's chore.

And it's true, I gather love
as others gather breath for tears
and I love the golden light that weighs
upon the petals of narcissus. I love
your cobalt skies, the lightness of air
you carry in your fists. You hold your head
as a daffodil regales in the sun. Let me be
summer for you, past the profusion of
weeds I once was when my brown soul
huddled in her winter grave of girlish earth.

IV

———

On the Fear of Going Down

Love. It's terrifying.
Why anything can happen.

—Jack Gilbert

On Locomotion

for Jay

If I gave you release you wouldn't like it,
the petit mal of passengers on an all night
journey, the giving it up of letting it all
go, the slack-jawed mouth opening, deaf
joints or fish flesh cooked to perfection.

It takes less than a minute to fall in love,
less time than it takes to scale a dollar
of dimes from a salmon, than anger's
claw or grasping a fish stunned under
a boulder's tumbling waterfall.

If I fed you would you metaphor
into blossoms of cheek blush,
would you flourish and survive
on a Grecian sea, chopping the wood
of Seferis? Would you fill

on French fried sardines and harden
into countryside, into the infinite beauty
of waves and the impeccable blue
of what mirrors light on the filled
significance of the empty?

The light was unbearably living
as the dark is unbearably dead, shattered
as the exploded pods of weeds; the sear
of your eyes in a dim room, an ignition
of spark, of steamer flare on rail.

Walking Around

for Jay

"It's the waves," he says, "the closest
I've ever come to eternity
is the ocean." It's the closest
I've ever been to infinite desire
and the fulfillment of salt.
I was born here. I've got brine
in my billowing hair. I've got grit
enough for a continent.
There's a foundation here
beneath the gentle lapping
of the have and have not
of distance; there's a horizon
of difference here, Plymouth Rock
under the shoal and the balein
from migrating whales, the gentle
ignorance of natural selection.
Tell me some things. Tell me
about travels and the Ark of your
baggage. You can ballast the levee
with the blastings. Slag,
cut to a fine aperture,
is as good a master as not.
This I know. Deceit tells its tale.
It's winter. The heartbeats
of sea lions pound into the wood
of the pier. On the rock
the golden wolves' eyes catch
the searchlight of the lighthouse.
They can't help it, for the look
of the light drives them
to this blind alley where I walk,
heavy with the towing of ancestors,
along the coast where my grandmother's
grandmother dived for oysters
now extinct. I can't see them,
but the eyes tell all
they're there, lounging

in their velvet pajamas.
Lords of an element but dumb
to the light that blinds them,
that reveals them now in the flesh.
Precious few have seen it.
Fewer among them have touched it
past the kelp. Fish eye
the boats, masters of none
but the palate. I watch
the stolid seals preen their blond
whiskers. I see the sleekness
of their leap onto the pilings
and wonder at impossible
distance and the weight of things.
That cloud bank, for instance,
the darkness behind it that's
either storm or a trail.
We could walk, I say,
we could let go
these horses and watch
the waves of their hooves
fly eternally into a sunset.
That's what was said,
before the cavalries came,
Walk with me, will you?
You and I walk.

Continental Divide

for Jay

If X were a stream leading clear
to Y and your lips were aspen
leaves falling, falling as a heart
balks above the precipice of winter,
there would be no divide, no
division of time between the breath
of your goodbye and the fine
crust of this distance between us,
and I would be the first to break
the ice of your longing, Persephone
returned, lugging her pomegranates
disguised as a young woman's breasts.
I would hold you as I hold
my longing now, still, enveloped
in dewlap folds, a crease of doubt
in the thunderhead. No, Pluto, you
are better cast as seed. Here,
let the white netherland gorge
unroll from your window. Let it be
my window sill. I will lean.
I will need if you need me. Pull
your ballads from the darkness
to the light of zoneless flesh.
We were brought here to stare down
the beast. You will butcher. I will
tan the hide the color of my skin.
I will teach you secrets, what never
wastes. We will walk. We will
fish. Here, Neptune, together
we shall stick the knife into
the carapace, split the claw
and ladle in every direction.

Buckshot

For now it is September
And the killing has begun.

—an old Irish folk song

My man wants to kill.
He longs to shoot his guns into the air
sacs of still steaming breath. He tries
to heave himself into the sight
and narrow his anger into a new
dimension. My love wants to stun
the living daylights out of creation,
hang the dead ruff in keening
wind and break the wings
as rigor mortis sheds the feathers
easily into his fine and slender hands.

In the season of the dark spill
I see him shiver on the rill, and feel
his dogs' tense happiness, smell
the blood spoor of his wolf and hair
matted and close as after sex. His toes
are cold as bullets in the blind. The siren
of his eyes as taut as cat gut as he

                            waits.

My sullen angler performs his task
with attention all his own as if in sleep.
His murmured cell of breath escapes
a life of smoke within the mist. He gives
the added slack, pulls the line in sentences,
in the Morse code of fish, a diddled dance
of prey. He settles for my cold blood
but counts the nights before his holiday
of death.

Shooting the Wren

For ten centuries I want to be birdless

—Jay Griswold

He sends trophies from Sunday's kill: a China
pheasant—feathers despicable starling coal,
backs the color of Chilean copper. They shimmer
in the distance, *a beautiful expectancy of only 2.2*
years so who could feel bad about the downing
of another rooster? The species about wiped out
for the hats of the thirties are plentiful
game now. They succumb to harsh winters,
feral cats, coyotes, wild dogs, farmers. The hens
preen in the spattered leaves. A speckle of blood,
nearly unnoticed, backs the wolf-down, and at
the quill's tip, a dark tangling in the fluff
of a ringneck's queue. They gleam iridescence,
what was more precious than gold to an extinguished
race. I walk among the ghosts of history, the
agony of the tortured condemned to their barracks
of serene mustard slopes. In California: China
berry, manzanita, wild boar imported from Europe.
My ancestors leached acorns, hollowed granite
at river beds with kindness kneading in a steady
procession. My grandmother knew only one
constellation, the Seven Sisters, and she would
ask them to help her remember her grandmother's
story of how they descended to earth from
a fusion of difference. But it's an unremembered
song cut off at slavery's beck and call. Her
eleven year old hands deadened at the hard
sale of cash, unlikely, untutored, caring.
She taught me the rights of a hunter are inalienable,
spinning the head of a chicken. It is true.
We are the fallen angels returned to teach
the tenderness of hands, the tough choice
of heart. My grandmother's heart was pure as topaz.
She knew what gives out comes back quantum.
She taught her babies patience with the eye

of a feather smudged with honey. A day's work
could get done as the plume was passed from hand
to hand in the brilliance of sunlight, bright
as it is now as I finger the fray
and nap of this gift.
                                    You are of the tender
heart. I know nothing of your hands but what
they write down, what graphite is bound between
horizons of blue, what nature of carbon skin
of dead birds coats the page. It is true. You can
buy the lean meat of plucked birds. You can buy
fresh hens at the market, quail the color of
chardonnay grapes. You have reservations where
you can purchase the tokens of the dead. They bear
their own speeches, these silent ones
trading the winds, their own histories and stories.
Tell me a few. Give it 2.2 years to come to life
and tell a tale of triggers and steel, of tumblers
and the slut peg of the chamber; mail me a silver
bullet from the mountains of your memory.
Your trophies bear witness to gunfire in the
numbed trees of eternity's forests, of winter
in the eastern plains—while I fashion
these feathers into the fragile art of my tribe.
I will wear them when the black of white
never dies, this gift of intent woven in a silent
bead. I'll let it blow through my matted
locks, the weight of a kiss. What you kill
I will pray for, what you let live
we will praise, ignore it, and eat.

Point Lobos

for Jay

If it's kindness you crave, here's the soft
ash of the hardest wood I've scavenged. Drifts
complete the reams of smoke billowing off
your knotted eyes. My hardest year was autumn
before the ban on burning, when what teared
my eyelids was the leaving of what sticks fast
in rip. I skim a surface grace, a shoal now hard
as ash, more brilliant in the shine than aspens
on the dark rills of your western slope. Before
a winter wash I come upon this shore where grebe
and egret print the beach in black and white,
and the stucco of my days unglues the tile
remembrance in this wet and ice and stolid fire.
I know the gentlest down, incorporated on a ridge
where something hungers, green to the breastbone
red patch at the throat like what mistakes you,
singing, for a flower. For this the shallows
give up ghosts, and what's glued up tight
as shell unfolds hunger in the black grit
of a tide embarked on patterns in a
shell-shocked sky. The iridescence
of my age glistens me in on this weathered
wood I cling to, and opens when the crash
collapses against a man as soft as sand,
stone, engraved, with hearts and names
that wear in wind. My open edge
expires on a season's dusk, in red
lips of thunderhead upon a blue shell,
pearled, found, and full of wonder,
of you, of smoke, this kind of ash.

The Last Meal

Towards midnight our bodies turn into themselves.
The cupboards open, hands help themselves to things,
small bowls of beluga, strawberries, sweet kernels
of luck, nippled and sunned under nightlight. Thick
hunger catches them, turns them to breath. They
breathe in scents of kitchen spices, auras of basil,
released ticklings of nutmeg, coriander, unexpected
openings of orange, dusks, dawn's harvested moons.
Intact, and beaming over fields of musk poppies,
amaranth and maize, they're pulling in the nets,
the fresh haul, the first scent.

Fisherman

for Jay

My love sleeps best
beside a brook or when
the ventricles of a heart
slush against his chest.

A steady rain now beats
upon our tent as he goes down
into that sound and comes up
dripping and fighting for breath.

He dreams fish the size
of bulldogs and he dives
into himself at night, deceived
by the shallow ridge of flesh

where there is no end, no bottom-
land to plant his bony seed,
only the lull of the quest, just
the shadow he sees pulling him

under into that greener state
where he nests the speckled trout
in the gold cups of his glimmering
palms. He's happiest in the pull

coaxing his line up from
the depths, penetrating
the interior, that inner green
circular hiding where the dead

chortle and gurgle like
carp in the alluvial debris
scribbling messages in the mud
for those still breathing in

the invisible air. He is this movable
element, visible upon the currents
of the dark, an intelligent wind,
a stalk of wild grass; he goes now

over the parched knoll
to the bend in the river fork.
Someday he will find his golden
shoes of fish fins, take the rippling

gill between his fingers, spread its
lips, and discover what is written
there in the land between bloodlines,
riverbeds; and something will

speak an unhearable tone, a trophy
of throat and slime. And his lines,
the taut parachute silks of his fall,
will weave themselves into a bridge,

a crossing into life,
the greatest death of all.

On Finding the Slide of John
in the Garden, 1973

Half my life I have slept beside a man
cradling his slender bowl of body between
my wheat. I have dreamed into his pillow
and he, sunk deep into that cylinder of my other
heart, would beat with the traded ritual of mutual
moons. I have waxed and waned within the single
shadow of his cleft and our bloodburn mingled
and ashed into the calligraphy of a landscape
left or vanished into giving. There are acres
of seeds we have swept into a shaft as the picket
fence of daybreak/dusk, the sincere sets of white and
black, marked breadth. We have lived our dreaming
awkwardly at best. We did not pause to reflect
but danced fast and in staccato as characters
splayed upon the silver of some aging screen.
There would be no turning back as the ratchet
of our distinct and distant hearts buries itself
against the pawl: one turned the wheel, one slams
the door, an engine guns itself of summer. Gone.

Half a life lived listening, bearing witness to the lapping
faucet drip within the furred nectar of his chest.
Half a heart, womb-sunk, misted, steaming opened
entrails in his midst. Now a cool sun sets frost
upon the silken strands of corn fifteen years picked.
Now he stands before the blonding stalks, stunned
in the focus of an unprojected slide. I can hold him
to the flailing sun and see him gold again and flush
with the grimace of pleasure, a stirring satisfaction
in the shovel spooning earth to feed. It would appear
as such, again ignited with that inner, first
married light, that other knowing, growing, love.

Half my life, in time, a third. I wait beside
a book, before my cooling coffee and the coal
slow icing of my hair, and the place would be
blank where once he stood and held, where he sleeps

alone now, inundating as a dream, recurred,
reorganized into a picture, that certain look decaying
into sunset rusts. A quarter life—it will come to pass.
A fifth or sixth of it if I dare not stop the steeping
breath rasp. Until finally, stilled and spinning
down to wire, it will surface, old nightmare
ascension, the emptiness of flowered desire;
my half-life, final delivery, a shucked single
kernel of care, my *you and me* transparency.

On the Last Anniversary

Here in an immense forest of winter
I think of you as a bird barely missed
but noticed in the armory of distance.
Dazzling as Da Nang your first virgin fall,
the sarongs of autumn popularize the countryside,
huge sides of color lengthen the Flatirons,
burglaries of purples and wine clot the foliage
of my first life without you, here, where the picture
puzzles fuse into the refuse of my calendar
drift. Pumpkins, aspen, sumac hold their brush
to the painted mirrors of the virtuous ponds.
Like women they enfold upon themselves as they
age. They become fertile as grass, then asphyxiating
as the cold clear eye of the season's last
lake—amphibious and killing. It lifts my vision,
solitaire, chosen and found. I'm caught again
by a stolen joy, by love, by absence.

Where you are the willow never yellows in December.
Here the owl's final visage soars and clamps
about the rippling muscles of rodents. Toads
in the marsh smell swell and belly curl their
mimicry of distant cows lowing their love
cries from the herd. You are no love of mine,
yet you are a persistent barking from the kennels.
Hear them running on the wire? They're testing
the measure: I'm one thousand miles without you.
Here, where winter pleases me, where the sunsets
of my youth happen and a light as fine
as my puzzled march through time seizes
me leaping the turnstile—I know
I will go on in this life, without you.

On the Fear of Going Down

Man owns four things that are useless at sea:
rudder, anchor, oars, and the fear of going down.

Pity the man who sees the water running and says,
'The thirst I have cannot be quenched by drinking.'

—Antonio Machado

Boats on the bay cull the willing
daggers of fins and fishtails, sleek
in the wake of the breaking tide.
They swell with light as sails
slap and the lockets and chains chime
Chinese music in the pentameter
winds. We are going down
where the sun first cut apart
a horizon of olives, ice and bruises
now opening with the shark's teeth
of spring. A light as fine as
the line of bone on the ridge
of your nose appears, a beacon,
a quest, resting on miles of shallows,
and the winding of signal begins
its descent. Cover me, will you?

The set sun gives out and comes
away all painted mercury. Plunged
in the coal of insomnia's shadow, I emerge
like the face in the vase no one sees.
The smell of your sleep going down
or the mark of your skin when
my pressing has left lies
persistent as the promise
of rain. And what if age should
knead my face to a handsome
dime? Or the blusters of winter
whittle my black linen nest
at the nape of my neck longing
for your errant kiss?

I sleep alone and count the night's
lean ribs. Thirty six twigs at the foot
of this shaking tree, forty two beatings
of my sudden heart fall before your
sword of daffodil oozes yellow light
from the line of my emptiness, dawning,
and the stalled hulk at the road
sounds a warning, an owl's breath
calling out fog or the terror
of blindness, passing.

And my heart, what of these boats
who have nowhere to go but the sea?
And the sea which has nothing
to share but the lives we pull
from her gullet? Hide them again
from my sight, these wooden buoys,
these stick sailors going down
for the final count.

I wear you like a love
that is really a sweater. I love
you like the filling of slough.
I don't know where to take off
above the barren ghost trees
at the heart of your river or
if my wings would hold
more wind than a sleeve.
Could you tell the pilings
have shattered? And the decay,
does it come to you brittle at
hand as a sound that falls silent?

We are going down. There, where
whales break water and the bears
who have returned to an element
they once despised ride hunger
beneath the bows now loaded
for arrival. They are leaning
on their nets. They are taking
what comes to them: the catch
of their lives is the sea.